BEACH
DEVOTIONS

refreshing your soul with
lessons from the beach

by Laura Vae Gatz

Editors: Elizabeth Grimm, Rob DeLanoy and Don & Joanne Gatz
Cover Design & Photographs, Interior Photographs
and Design: Laura Vae Gatz

http://lauragatz.com
facebook.com/LauraVaeGatz

CONTENTS

for my husband, Rob, my gift from God,
who inspires me to draw closer
to Christ everyday

ADIRONDACK CHAIRS

And the peace of God, which surpasses all understanding,
will guard your hearts and your minds in Christ Jesus.

PHILIPPIANS 4:7

As I write this I'm sitting on the couch, looking outside at the snow silently falling straight down, in big flakes, through the bare trees and evergreens that line our backyard, which backs up to the forest. It's peaceful and beautiful, and yet makes me long for summertime and long afternoons on the patio. I love to sit there, in an Adirondack chair, with a journal or book at hand, and possibly a bottle of water for when I get thirsty. There's something about an Adirondack chair that just says "summer – camp – relaxation" to me. I love the bright colors they are often painted, although a bright blue chair with white arms is my favorite because that is the color the Adirondack chairs were painted at camp when I was a child. I love the broad arm rests that are perfect for resting my arms on or for placing a few books, drinks and snacks on. I can sit for hours, with my feet propped up on a railing in front of me, listening to the waves crash on the beach, and to the delightful laughter and giggles of children playing on the swing set and running in and out of the waves. And right now, looking at the snow falling, I can feel that immense peace and joy that of those sunny Shangri-La afternoons.

Afternoons like that remind me of how God is in control of everything - even the waves. It can be hard to realize that the waves crash on the beach whether I'm there to hear them or not. And God is with me whether I feel His presence or not. God is in control of everything. It's sort of like knowing the sun is up there, behind the clouds, even if we haven't seen it in days.

I wish I would always feel that solid sense of assurance; that I would be able to feel that warm, comforting feeling, as if God has scooped me up in His arms and is giving me a big, long hug. But it doesn't always happen. And that's often my fault.

When I get busy in the midst of the craziness of life and don't make time for God, that's when I lose the peace in my heart. When I mentally shut Him out of my day because I don't want to face the real issue at the heart of my problem or current concern, that's when the day's troubles start looking overwhelming and impossible. But as soon as I turn to the Lord, and ask His help to make it through, then my peace returns even if the problem hasn't been resolved. That is because I know He is with me through everything and with God I know all things are possible.

I work hard to build those "Adirondack chair moments" into my daily life. It takes perseverance, and when I veer off course and feel the consequences of drifting off target, I must correct my course and get back "in the chair." Most mornings before I ever roll out of bed I listen to a podcast devotional from one of my favorite preachers. Sometimes it's a two-podcast day because I'm having a particularly difficult time getting motivated to face the day. When I commuted to work I often listened to devotional radio broadcasts on the way to and from the office. In the evening I'm reading my way through the Bible and I even keep a small Bible in the bathroom for those daily breaks as well. Find what works for you. And then keep doing it especially when you feel that you are drifting away.

Dear Lord, So often it can be hard to keep the peace I found while I was on vacation, away from the requirements of my daily life. Help me to recapture those moments by dedicating myself to spending time with You and in Your Word, daily. Send the Holy Spirit to prick my conscience when I drift away. Make me aware that the best times in my life are when I'm walking the closest with You. Amen.

DRIFTWOOD

But the pot he was shaping from the clay
was marred in his hands; so the potter formed it into another pot,
shaping it as seemed best to him.

JEREMIAH 18:4 NIV 2001

'm a beachcomber. I love nothing better than to walk on the beach and see what presents itself to me, whether a particularly smooth round rock, some beach glass or a piece of drift wood. There's something about driftwood that is wonderful. Like the rocks on the beach it's been tossed about by the waves, rolled around and worn smooth by the sand; it's something other than what it was when it first entered the water. Driftwood might start off as a plain and simple utilitarian 2x4 plank or maybe a branch that was swept into the water during a big storm, but something magical happens to it during its time in the water. It's changed by forces outside of its control. And when I find it washed up on the beach I find it beautiful; therefore I'm not usually thinking about the process it must have gone through to look this way. I'm just happy to have found it, and I turn it over to examine it, looking at the smooth finish or the interesting shape it has become.

I think that's how God is, with us. He takes something plain and unremarkable and turns us into His works of art through the trials in our lives. The loss of a job sands us smooth, calling on our faith to sustain us, knowing that God has a plan for our lives even if we can't see that plan at the moment. Sickness of a loved one tosses us about on emotional waves and causes us to draw closer to God as our world seems out of kilter and we feel a loss of control. Daily stresses are like a constant sand-blasting that smooths off our sharp edges and causes us to develop patience and perseverance. All these trials make us beautiful and conform us more to the image of Christ. In the middle of the storm, the last thing I'm thinking about is becoming a stronger person and a more "beautiful" person, but when the waves have calmed and the sun has come out again I'm always amazed to look back and see who I used to be and see what wonderous changes God has worked in me.

So when you feel like you're being tossed about by life's waves or being sanded smooth by rocks that seem to be in your path, stop and ask God to use those trials to strengthen you, to draw you closer to Him, and to align your will with His. Remember that He is always with us, and never more so than in the middle of our trials.

Lord, Thank You for the beauty of driftwood. Let it help us to remember that You are the potter, and we are the clay and that You are patiently molding us into the persons You would have us to be; stronger, closer to You, and with ever increasing faith in You through Your Son Jesus Christ. Amen.

RIPTIDES

*Trust in the LORD with all your heart; do not depend on your
own understanding. Seek His will in all you do,
and He will show you which path to take.*

PROVERBS 3:5-6 NLT 2007

As a kid I can remember being on the beach and looking longingly at the water, wanting to go in swimming, and having my mom or dad tell me, "No, you can't go in swimming yet. You have to wait for an adult to go into the water with you." Oh that was so frustrating! In my little kid's brain I was thinking, "The water is right there. What's going to happen? I know how to swim! Why can't I go in now? I want to go in now!"

As a child we are so unaware of all the dangers that could befall us in the water. We're not thinking of the dangers when we think about going in swimming by ourselves, only the fun and excitement. As adults, the dangers are so evident to us. We know that dangerous currents can exist that will suck even the strongest of swimmers out into the lake. We understand how easy it is to get into water that is too deep and get too tired to swim back. And then it's always possible that someone's boogie board could knock you in the head and you could lose consciousness for enough time in which to drown.

As adults we often act like those kids on the beach who want to go in swimming, *now*! We see an opportunity before us and we want to rush in, seeing only the benefits, and not stopping to consult our Father on what His will for our life may be. Sometimes it's so tempting!

This past year a job opportunity became available for my husband and we knew we had to stop to consult the Lord before arriving at an answer as to whether we were going to pursue it or not. We had already been praying for several months that the Lord would clearly show us where He would have us live and what job He would have my husband accept. At first the job sounded ideal, in just the location we would have chosen if we'd have been able to pick a town to live in, but both of us quickly could feel in our hearts and minds that it was not the right decision.

It's so easy to make a decision in life and not involve the Lord at all, and only later realize that the decision you made might not have been the decision God would have had you make. One of the benefits of walking closely with the Lord, reading His Word daily, and praying throughout the day, is the ability to more keenly feel His will for our lives. I can also tell, when I ask God for something I know is coming in the future, and ask that He align my will to His, that the decision making process is so much easier than it would have been if I hadn't been praying about it from before the start.

God only wants the best for us. In order for us to receive God's best we have to be open and available to walking in the path He would have us walk. And we have to trust Him. Sometimes that trust is easier to talk about than to put into action, I know! One way I combat the temptation to doubt God is by keeping a prayer journal into which I enter my prayer and a date, and then record God's answer along with a date. Seeing this history of answered prayer is such a testimony to how God has worked in my life and it renews my faith when I'm tempted to doubt God's plan.

Dear Lord, Thank You so much for being my loving Father, and for always wanting the best for me in my life. Please help me to wait on Your timing, and to refrain from rushing into a decision because I want something right away. Keep me close to You and encourage me to stay in Your presence by reading Your Word daily and by keeping You near me throughout the day as I pray about my daily concerns and offer praise to You for Your abundance of blessings. Amen.

KAYAKING

For I know the plans I have for you,
declares the Lord, plans for welfare and not for evil,
to give you a future and a hope.

JEREMIAH 29:11

Kayaking is one of my favorite ways to get outside and enjoy nature. Kayaking down a river poses different challenges than kayaking on a big lake. Paddling on Lake Michigan can be more like sea kayaking, where it's easy to feel the rise and the fall of the waves, and where the wind and current have a big influence in your direction. When I'm out in my blue kayak I like to feel like I'm in control, but as soon as a big wave or a particularly stiff wind blows my way, I realize it's only partly true. And when I figure in the bigger picture of life I realize it's only nominally true.

We all like to think we are in control: in control of what we're going to wear today, what we will eat, what path we choose to take to work, or how much we will accomplish in a given day. And sure, there's a degree of control in that, but we are certainly not in control of our lives; God is. And praise the Lord for that! There is so much comfort in that knowledge, especially when the wind is blowing hard in my face while I'm fighting to go the direction I want to go, or the waves of life are towering over me. God always wants the best for us, but sometimes we will have to go through trials in order to get to the blessings He has planned for us.

Growing up, my mom had small piece of handblown-glass hanging in the kitchen window with the image of a monkey hanging onto a branch. It said "Let go, and Let God." I've always remembered that phrase and I try hard to apply it when I feel myself trying to take control of situations in my life that I know I should give up to God. Sometimes I struggle to release my illusion of control and give an issue over to God; in fact many times I have to give the same thing to God over and over again because I keep taking it back.

One of the things that helps me the most is to review my prayer list from over the years. It gives me a history of the issues and requests I've made to God, and I can see over and over again how God is faithful and always answers my prayers, perhaps not in the way I thought He would, or with the timing I wanted Him to, but He does indeed answer. *"God causes all things to work together for good to those who love God, to those who are called according to his purpose (Romans 8:28)."* It's so wonderful to look back over my life to see how God orchestrated circumstances to make His will and His plan work out in my life. That history is part of my testimony to those I meet, and I look for openings in conversations which allow me to share how God is the author of my life.

Lord, thank You so much for the assurances in Your Word that You are in control of my life, and that no matter what trials and storms I am facing, You will bring good out of it. Help me to trust in Your faithfulness, and Your eternal love, and give me peace in my heart knowing that You are in control — of it all. Amen.

A Walk in the Woods

Therefore put on the full armor of God, so that when the day of evil comes, you may be able to stand your ground, and after you have done everything, to stand. Stand firm then, with the belt of truth buckled around your waist, with the breastplate of righteousness in place, and with your feet fitted with the readiness that comes from the gospel of peace. In addition to all this, take up the shield of faith, with which you can extinguish all the flaming arrows of the evil one. Take the helmet of salvation and the sword of the Spirit, which is the word of God. And pray in the Spirit on all occasions with all kinds of prayers and requests. With this in mind, be alert and always keep praying for all the Lord's people.

EPHESIANS 6:13-18 NIV 2011

A walk in the woods can be so refreshing. A nice change of pace from our usual lives which tend to keep us inside most of the time; jobs that keep us locked up in buildings which have windows that don't open, house chores that keep us inside dusting and doing laundry. I don't know about you, but I tend to feel better when I can get outside, breathe in the loamy smells of plants and evergreens, and get out of town, out of the subdivision and into God's great creation.

There is a forest behind my parents' cottage, just off the shore of Lake Michigan. In it are paths that I've traveled ever since I was a kid. As a kid there was always one cardinal rule to follow if I was going to be in the woods: wear a hat! Secondly, I was to tuck my pants into my socks so that ticks would only be able to crawl up the outsides of my pants, not the insides. Despite all the allure and charm of the forest, it always holds hidden dangers. In mothers' minds these dangers can be big enough to make us want to keep our kids out of the forest. The poison ivy is always a danger especially to little boys who don't want to take the time to look where they are walking before they walk there. The ticks are always present in the summer but this last summer they were especially bad and the possibility of contracting Lyme disease from them is very real.

Sometimes it's hard to equate a relaxing and enjoyable walk in the woods with danger. And it can be the same for our daily walk in the world. Unless we keep ourselves attuned to our Christian walk, the hidden dangers of the world can sneak up on us and infect us.

Ephesians 6 talks of "putting on the whole armor of God," as we venture out into this world that we live in. I think God knows that although we don't want to be "of this world," it is the only world we have to live in and therefore have to interact with it, at least in part.

The farther I deviate from what most of the world sees and does, the easier I can clearly see how the world is cunning and clever to deceive people from the truth. On the surface, watching TV seems so harmless but much of what is broadcast is shaping the beliefs and morals of our young people. I stopped watching television in 2007 and haven't missed it. Now when the TV does happen to be on, I'm appalled by what I see - the lack of morals and even the names of the shows: Pretty Little Liars, Revenge, Scandal, Cougar Town. I could go on. These names alone tell you that the show is not on moral high ground.

With this in mind, we need to carry the Lord with us wherever we go. Use our shield of faith to deflect the flaming arrows of the evil one. Put on the helmet of salvation. Use the sword of the spirit. Basically, filter our world through our Christ-colored glasses and not be fooled into believing the hype that the world evangelizes. The world's claims are empty and hollow. God's promises satisfy our hearts and minds, and are everlasting.

Dear Lord, This world can be so deceptively enticing and misleading. As we walk through our daily lives, whether it is in the woods or out in the world, please be our armor, which defends us from the sometimes-subtle attack from the evil one. Use our faith in You as our defense against ideas and beliefs which are contrary to Your teachings, and help us to protect our children from being misled, as well. Encourage us to use our time in activities pleasing to You. Amen.

LOST PETOSKEY

Do not lay up for yourselves treasures on earth, where moth and rust destroy and where thieves break in and steal, but lay up for yourselves treasures in heaven, where neither moth nor rust destroys and where thieves do not break in and steal. For where your treasure is, there your heart will be also.

MATTHEW 6: 19-21

When I was a young child, I was walking along the beach, looking for Petoskey stones with my sister and some friends. In addition to Petoskey hunting they were also finding flat rocks and skipping them out into the water. I found a particularly nice Petoskey and exclaimed, "Oh, I found a perfect one!" One of the older girls asked to look at it, and then to my horror, she reached back her arm, and before I could stop her, she used my perfect Petoskey as a skipping stone, and it was lost among the waves forever. I'm sure it was an honest mistake, but I was so upset. It's not easy to find a good Petoskey in Michigan in the summer. So many people are out looking for them that they become scarce. I felt the pain of losing my perfect find to which I'd already assigned great personal value.

Even though that loss was a very small one, and more than 30 years ago, I can still feel the pain of it. In our lives God sometimes asks us to give up something that we're holding on too tightly to, something that may have come to mean more to us than He does. It could be an object we highly prize, or it could be time that we jealously guard against intrusions. Or it could be an attitude we have about a person or an event from our past. If we can identify what God is asking us to give up, and realize that we may not be living within God's will for our lives in that specific area, we're now closer to making a positive change, and maturing in our walk with the Lord.

It's not easy. Things I hold onto tightly are typically within areas where I need to grow or learn a lesson, and it's not usually a lesson I relish learning. I've found that if I can pray about it, letting God know that I understand my need to change, even if I don't particularly want to change, it will start the change process. Have you heard the phrase "Fake it 'til you make it?" That can apply to prayer, as strange as that sounds. You don't have to feel the feeling in your heart in order to ask God for something. A lot of times the "need" starts with the knowledge of what needs to be done, long before you feel like doing it. Often I'll pray that God would change my heart and my desire and align them with His will for my life. Essentially I'm saying to God, "Yeah, I know I need to change but I can't quite pray for the change yet, but please initiate that change within me so that I want to make the change."

Dear Lord, Please make me aware of areas in my life that I need to let You into. Even if I don't feel as if I want to change, give me the awareness of my need to change and encourage me to ask You to change my will to be in sync with Yours. Show me the awesome blessings You have planned for my life, if only I'll surrender every part of my life to You. Amen.

BEACH COTTAGE

Do not love the world or the things in the world. If anyone loves the world, the love of the Father is not in him. For all that is in the world—the desires of the flesh and the desires of the eyes and pride in possessions—is not from the Father but is from the world. And the world is passing away along with its desires, but whoever does the will of God abides forever.

1 JOHN 2:15-17

A summer cottage on the beach evokes thoughts of cool breezes wafting in open windows, around cotton curtains, and well-worn hardwood floors, pictures from summers long-past hanging in the hallway, and the faded glory of the same Formica kitchen table and chairs that we used when I was a kid. Oh, and the sound of a screen door slamming. That really says summer and "lake" to me. Funny how a slightly annoying sound evokes so many fond memories!

The things I remember about our cottage have nothing to do with what it didn't have. I love it all the better and probably have more memories about the place because we didn't have a television, and air conditioning wasn't even a consideration. We all slept in one room, in two beds, separated by a curtain made out of a blanket.

What's that phrase – simple pleasures are the best? A cottage grows in our hearts and memories by the things that stay the same, the memories we create there, and by the stretches of time we spend there with friends and family sheltered by its simple walls and roof. I think cottage memories are often stronger than other memories not only because of the repetition of spending time there year after year and the annual friendships that develop, but because we're away from the routine of our lives, and cottage life is so often more simple than daily life: no bills to pay or phone calls to return, no work conference calls or laundry to do (well, at least not until we've been there a few days!). Our lives aren't focused on maintaining "things" or using technology, but on each other and on building relationships, spending time together, playing games in the evening.

As I describe life at "the cottage" I can't help but picture one of Norman Rockwell's paintings of picturesque life in the 1920's. And I think that's how God would have us strive to live, not striving for something perfect and unobtainable, but to live by keeping life as simple as possible, keeping our focus on the Lord and on each other, and not getting lost in what the world has to offer. Cottage life is a great template for how to live daily, as much as possible.

I think my daily mantra is reminiscent of some of the lines in the book *"Everything I know I learned in Kindergarten."* Mine goes: "Wake up early, pray to the Lord, stretch, eat breakfast, pray throughout the day. When I'm stressed out at the end of my workday, spend quiet time with God – don't turn on the TV! Walk, pray, sleep." Of course that isn't always attainable, but it is something I strive for, each day, one day at a time.

Dear Lord, Please help me to keep my life simple, and to keep You first in everything that I do. Send me that little internal voice that tells me to read the Bible, stop to pray, and to stop everything and just listen for Your voice. Encourage me to reach out to others and maintain the heart of a servant; thinking of others before I think of myself. I love You so much. Amen.

Riding the Wave

Therefore, my beloved brothers, be steadfast, immovable, always abounding in the work of the Lord, knowing that in the Lord your labor is not in vain.

I Corinthians 15:58

This last summer, at the ripe old age of 40-something, I experienced boogie boarding for the first time. What a rush! Although I'd seen my nephews do it down in Florida a few years ago I hadn't really ever thought about doing it myself until my husband brought out a few boards one particularly wavy day this summer on Lake Michigan. We had a blast! It is so much fun to wait for the right wave; making sure to be in the right spot, and then to push off with your legs and ride the wave a long time until it peters out, and you do it all over again. It's certainly a great way to get exercise, almost without knowing it.

What a great feeling it is to be caught up in the wave, surfing on top of it – or slightly in front of it. I almost feel as if I'm flying. When I catch the wave in just the right spot, and I'm surfing along, I feel as if I'm part of the wave. One of the best parts is when I can find a stationary reference point, like a person in the water standing still, in order to be able to see just how fast and far I'm traveling. Once the wave has fizzled out and I stand up, I'm amazed at how far the wave has taken me.

One of the hardest parts about boogie boarding for me is standing up after the ride is over. Where we boarded this summer there was a sand bar a good 10 yards off the beach. I would head out past the sand bar to catch each wave, and then end up back on the sand bar in water about a foot deep or less. It's a hard thing to get to my feet quickly when I'm basically lying horizontally on the beach, on top of a long board. If I don't get up before the next wave washes in it unbalances me and it's easy to fall over. I also find it hard to go from that wonderful feeling of weightlessness in the water to bearing the full weight of my body again as I stagger to stand upright.

Have you ever noticed how after a great weekend or vacation, that Monday, that first day back at work, can be a really rough day? It's as if the more fun you had, the harder it is to come back to reality. The experience can feel similar to that feeling of standing up out of the water at the end of a wild ride. The weight of my body feels like more than I can bear. Reality seems too stark.

I've found that after some great times in my life, be it a great vacation, a promotion, or simply a long stretch of contentment, sometimes I feel down in the dumps afterwards and it's hard to get my feet back under me. That happens mostly when I've stopped walking in sync with the Lord during those good times. It's easy to do. Life is great, I don't feel like I need to lean on the Lord, my prayer times diminish, and my focus changes from what would please Him to what would please me.

God knows that too many good times can lead us astray. When is it that you learn to walk more closely with God – is it during those good times? Nope. It's during trials and heartaches. That's when we grow, strengthening our faith. I know I need to keep reading God's Word daily everyday, no matter what's going on in my life. On vacation I have to keep having my daily devotional and not get distracted by all that there is to see and do. And I want to long to praise God for all His wonderful blessings in my life. Learning this balance can be hard. Each time I lose my balance I find myself evaluating where I made a wrong turn, and it quickly brings me back into closer relationship with my Lord and Savior.

Dear Lord, Keep me mindful of You and Your will for my life, both during trials and the good times. Help us to rely on You to hold us up in the waters of contentment and on the dry land of daily living. When I waver or wander off Your path, let the Holy Spirit prick my conscience and bring me back into the fold. Amen.

HEAT AND HUMIDITY

Beloved, do not be surprised at the fiery trial
when it comes upon you to test you,
as though something strange were happening to you.

1 PETER 4:12

Oh no, it's one of those days. The days I wish weren't part of summer. I'm at the beach; it should be perfect beach weather, not this hot, humid, stagnant day with no air moving at all. The oppressive heat makes me feel like I'm drowning in my own hot breath. There's no air conditioned room or building I can duck into for a brief reprieve. Bugs are buzzing around my head, delighting in my glistening skin. They're driving me nuts! This day seems never ending. A trial. The sand is so hot it burns the bottom of my feet. I've drunk all the water I brought with me. Even the lake water is so warm it's not refreshing. This day feels like a trial to slog through.

Days like these are part of any summer and can be likened to a desert time in our lives. A time of trial. A period I don't want to go through but want to get to the end of as soon as possible. Inevitably these hot and humid days of life tend to sneak up on me and take me by surprise. And it's so easy to slip into a bad attitude about it and stay there, never thinking to turn to God or ask for His assistance. This is where having friends in the Faith or a Godly spouse can be so helpful as they can hold me accountable for my thoughts and actions. They can ask me what's wrong and care enough to find out if I've prayed about the situation or if I've been reading God's word.

I'm simply amazed (over and over again) at how turning to God and reading the Bible changes my attitude so quickly. My circumstances haven't necessarily changed, but my reaction to them has. Once I have God's perspective, it's like a cool breeze has just caressed my face and dried the sweat from my brow. All of a sudden that trial that was weighing on me seems lighter, the day a bit brighter, and I don't notice the small annoyances any more.

We may prefer sunny, low humidity days in our lives, but those uncomfortable days are when our relationship with the Lord has the opportunity to be strengthened. Use the hot and humid days in your life as your chance to use all your God-given resources to grow closer to your Lord.

Dear Lord, I don't like the feeling of hot and humid days outside any more than I like the feeling of a hot and fiery trial that comes my way. Help me to take advantage of those times by turning to You immediately and asking for Your help to make it through. Be that cool breeze that refreshes me and changes my perspective in the midst of trials. Amen.

BEACHCOMBING

Be still and know that I am God...
PSALM 46:10

Beachcombing is so fascinating to me. I love to see what has washed up on the beach. There is an endless supply of rocks to explore and consider, and the rare bit of polished glass or smooth driftwood. Walking on the beach slowly, with my head down, focused on the treasures that present themselves along the way, is one of the ways that I unwind and slip out of my day-to-day life. I find it's much like reading a really good book; it takes me out of my immediate life and transports me to a place where there are no responsibilities or duties. My worries fade away and are replaced by fascination and curiosity. I'm amazed at the huge variety of rocks...their sizes, shapes, textures and colors. And there's always the elusive Petoskey to identify in the midst of all the other rocks!

Sometimes when I go to the beach with my husband we have to define our walk before we start it. Are we walking for exercise, or is this a beach-combing mission? The answer completely changes the walk. You have to walk slowly in order to find the best stuff on the beach. I think beachcombing can be a form of meditation; a way of slowing life down, eliminating extraneous thoughts from my mind, and of living in the moment. Everything else in life fades away, my breathing becomes more regular, and I have one focus — to find interesting items left on the beach either by the waves or by a person.

God calls us to slow down and be still. It's usually pretty hard for most people. I know when I've realized I need to spend time reading the Bible, it still takes me a long time to settle down and get to reading it. It's funny how I can know what I need to do and spend so much time avoiding it, seemingly unconsciously. Most of the time I read the Bible on an app on my iPhone, and I'll read it before I go to sleep at night or before I get out of bed in the morning. A typical night, when I know I plan to read the Bible goes like this: I get into bed with my iPhone, and before I open up the Bible app I decide I'm going to check my email, then I decide I'm going to get caught up on Facebook, and after that I make sure that all my apps are up to date. Eventually, after at least 10-15 minutes, I get down to business and start reading the Bible. Why, despite our best efforts is it so difficult to do what we want to do when it comes to drawing closer to God? Whether it's the devil or the world, without laser-focus it's so easy to drift off the path we mean to be on.

Roman 7:19 kind of applies here: *For I do not do the good I want, but the evil I do not want is what I keep on doing.* And verse 20 goes on to say that if we do the evil we do not want that it is no longer I who do it but sin that dwells within me. I suppose that's it. The things we want to do that are good are affected by the sin in our lives.

Each day I have to try again to do the things I want to do – the things I know I should do. It's like getting back on a horse that has bucked me off time and time again. Until we're in heaven with the Lord I suspect it's always going to be somewhat of a trial to do the good we want to, but building good habits and making a ritual time to do those good habits, can help. If I always read the Bible before I go to sleep I think I'll have a better chance of getting to it each night because I will have formed a habit. The trick is getting back into the habit if I break it and stop doing it. I also find that slowing down enables me to be more focused and less distracted by the world and when I'm less distracted by the world, I tend to be more focused on God because there's not quite as much vying for my attention. I will continue to work on being still, and spending more time with my Lord.

Dear Lord, Sometimes I find it hard to feel close to You each day. The world creeps in despite my better efforts to keep it at bay. Please work in my heart to keep You the focus in my daily life and help me to keep in Your Word, reading it daily. When I stray off the path You want me on, please gently nudge me back on the Your path. Amen.

SAND IN MY EYE

...let us pursue what makes for peace and for mutual upbuilding.
ROMANS 14:19

My mother is always amazed at how much sand finds its way into our front hallway in our beach cottage. I'm not quite as amazed by it; if you live at the beach, sand is part of life. My favorite thing to do when I first get to the beach each year is to take off my socks and shoes and run through the sand, feeling the texture and temperature of it envelop my feet. The combination of the texture and the temperature is unique and is such a wonderful feeling and memory from years of coming to the lakeshore.

When I'm at the beach on a windy day, I am immediately affected if one piece blows in my eye. One grain of sand is so small, but it can be so powerful. The same holds true if I get a piece of sand in my mouth while I'm out playing in the waves. I crunch on it and know immediately what it is. Finding it with my tongue and getting it out of my mouth is usually no easy job. As soon as I think I've gotten it out, I crunch on it again.

In the same way that one piece of sand can be so powerful if found somewhere unwelcome, the same holds true with sand dunes. Together, all those grains of sand have the power to overwhelm a forest as the wind moves each grain of sand slowly inland. Over time sand dunes can completely "drown" a forest. Each year at the beginning of the season I wander down to one of our beaches and am always amazed at how the walkway to the beach has been flooded by several feet of sand.

Just like a grain of sand, we can have a huge impact on the lives of those around us. Not just by what we say, but by how we act. Our strongest witness can be completely silent; we don't have to use words at all. In the same way, the way we live, and respond to circumstances, can have a powerful impression on those who know us.

The impact we have can be positive or negative. One misspoken word said to a child in anger can stay with them for a lifetime, like a grain of sand in the mouth that we can't wash out. On the flip side, a kind word or action towards a loved one or stranger can also have a lasting influence.

Be aware of your actions and their unseen results. When you feel the irritation building inside of you, before reacting, bow your head, at least mentally and ask the Lord for patience and the right words and actions to deal with the situation. And if you do loose your cool, once you've regained it, go back to the person it affected to ask their forgiveness. That kind of action can drown a forest of bitterness and resentment, and demonstrate God's love and grace shining in our lives. It might even be a good illustration to reference as you're sitting down to apologize; that as you are asking for their forgiveness, we in turn ask God to forgive us when we sin. And God, in His mercy and grace, always forgives us, time after time after time.

Lord, Please open my eyes to how I influence others by my actions, even those I do not know. Help me to be a shining light for Your Kingdom in my everyday life. And when I give in to temptation and negative emotions, encourage me to turn back to those I've hurt and to ask their forgiveness. Thank You for Your love and continual steady grace in my life and help me to extend that grace and love to others. Amen.

COOKOUT

*Give, and it will be given to you. Good measure, pressed down,
shaken together, running over, will be put into your lap. For with
the measure you use it will be measured back to you.*

LUKE 6:38

One of the great traditions at camp is the cookout. Once a week dinner would be served outside, usually on the same day that we had "half-day-out-of-camp" and went on a canoe trip. As a kid, I looked forward to the cookout with great relish. Back in the day, the cook, Gert, and all her workers, would make hamburger buns from scratch. Oh my! They were good! There would be home made potato salad, all the hamburger fixins', a big 5 gallon tin full of potato chips, and huge tins full of home made cookies: chocolate chip and double chocolate rebels! Oh, I can still taste the flavor of those cookies; the crunch of home made cookies, and the aroma of all those cookies sitting in a tin together. Truly a dream for a child who loved cookies like the cookie-monster!

We never had to worry if there would be enough to feed everyone. Because the staff knew how many people there were attending camp each week, they knew how to plan and always planned for more than enough to feed everyone – even all those very hungry canoe-trippin' adults and kids. So there was never a worry in my mind about if I would have enough to eat. The worry was more about if I might eat too much! Just as the staff at camp took care of the guests, we can trust the Lord to take care of us. God's provision for our lives is SO much more abundant.

In Matthew 6 the Bible says, *"Don't worry about your life, what you will eat or drink; or about your body, what you will wear...the birds of the air do not sow or reap or store away in barns, but My heavenly Father takes care of them..."* I sometimes find it can be hard to understand how to take those words and translate them into how I should act. Over the years I've come to realize that Jesus meant that if I concentrate on walking in God's Will, giving of my time and money, that God will take care of me. It's so opposite of what the world teaches which is "take care of yourself because no one else will."

This last year I've changed from tithing my take home pay to tithing my gross pay. At first I thought, "That's a lot of money, how will I make ends meet?" But the more I thought about it I realized that it ALL belongs to God, and He has blessed me with enough income to be able to make a difference, albeit a small one, in the world. I have increased my tithe and God continues to provide for all my needs. Time and time again, during those periods when I give more than usual, God is faithful and blesses me with more than I started out with - a living example of the parable of the talent (Matthew 25:14-30)! The philosophy of the world says "Give more when you have more." God says, "Give more and I will provide you more."

Dear Lord, Thank You for being such a loving and giving God. Thank You for taking care of us even when we stray from Your side. Use us to further Your Kingdom and to operate out of Your philosophy, not the world's. Increase our faith so we can comprehend how You will bless us as we bless others. Amen.

STORMS

And He awoke and rebuked the wind and said to the sea, "Peace! Be still!" And the wind ceased, and there was a great calm.

MARK 4:39

I love to watch a storm roll across the lake. How wondrous to see its raw power, and to watch the lightning and feel the thunder reverberate in my chest. I remember sitting on a cement ledge overlooking the beach, watching one storm roll in, many summers ago. Across almost the entire lake was a huge roll cloud. It looked like a big rolled up towel, horizontal in the sky. It continued to grow larger and come closer. Eventually we could see the line of rain as it swept across the lake towards us. And although we had been measuring the progress of the storm, it took us by surprise and all of a sudden we were in the middle of the terrible wind and sheets of rain. I stood up and ran for a building but before I got there every inch of me was soaked and covered with grains of sand. It was an exciting, if messy, experience. One I still remember in vivid detail today.

Storms can be fun to watch when they are far off, and even relatively close, but it's no fun to be in the middle of a storm when you're standing outside. They can be terrifying! The same goes for the storms of life. When it's someone else's life that is having the storm, it's easy to give advice and pray for them, but when it's my own life, and I'm personally experiencing the storm, that is a different matter. Suddenly it doesn't seem so easy to solve, and it's usually not fun to experience. The fascination melts away and my thoughts turn to worry. How long is this going to last? Am I going to make it through? Why me? What am I supposed to learn from this?

That last question is the key. Typically God has a purpose in the storms He allows into our lives. He doesn't cause them, but because we live in a sinful world and have hearts ruled by sin, He uses them to draw us closer to Him. The sooner we can learn the lesson, the sooner the storm will be over, at least sometimes.

I've learned to see the beauty in some of my life's storms (certainly not all of them – I'm still working on that!). When my sister was sick with Lymphoma for months on end, there were times where, despite the debilitating tiredness I experienced from worry, I was able to praise God in the midst of it all. There were so many blessings that my family and I experienced during that time. I know my faith grew stronger during that time. I ached for the trial to be at an end, for all of us, but I could see the sun poke out briefly from time to time, and it cast an amazing rainbow on our circumstances. I've never felt God's presence so acutely as when I was at my lowest.

Eventually the sun will come out from behind the clouds and our personal storm of the moment will pass. If we turn to Him, God will get us through storms in our lives, and we'll come out of it stronger and more Christ-like than when we started. Sometimes at the end of the storm we'll feel broken, but like broken glass tossed and turned by the waves and pounded into the sand, we'll end up being a beautiful piece of beach glass. Going through storms…makes us beautiful. And once we're on the other side and the storm is receding into the past, we can turn around and admire its beauty and thank God for the lessons we learned while we were in the middle of it.

Dear Lord, When storms come into my life, draw me closer to You. Encourage me to lean on You, seek the lesson in the storm, and use Your love, peace, patience and courage to face it. I know that through You I can do all things, even if I'd rather avoid the storm or have it just disappear. Help me to accept the trials of this life and use them as a force to draw closer to You. Amen.

LIGHTHOUSES

For just as the heavens are higher than the earth, so My ways are higher than your ways and My thoughts higher than your thoughts.
ISAIAH 55:9 NLT 2007

Lighthouses fascinate me. I love the history attached to them and the difficult and often lonely lives of those who cared for them. Some of my favorites include Point Betsie Lighthouse attached to the beautiful lightkeeper's house, just north of Frankfort, Michigan, the little Mackinac Island Lighthouse with its red and white brickwork, and the little Ushuaia Lighthouse in Argentina, very close to Cape Horn.

Lighthouses dot beautiful and dangerous sections of coast around the world. A few summers ago I spent some time around the Arctic Circle, and our ship stopped at a small island at the mouth of the White Sea. It housed a lighthouse painted black and white like the one at Cape Hatteras, North Carolina. It was very tall. I know, from photographs I saw of the island, taken from the top of that lighthouse, that the perspective from the top is completely different than the perspective from the ground. No, I never made it up to the top of that lighthouse. I started up the stairs, but remembered how heights make me feel and I opted for the safety of the ground.

Just as I couldn't climb to the top of that lighthouse, I also can't understand God's perspective. God's vastness and omniscience is so incomprehensible to me that I simply cannot understand His ways and His plan for my life. I know that God wants the best for my life and has a plan for it and if I stay in His word, and follow His will for my life, He will unfold the blessings He has stored up for me, in His time.

But sometimes that is so much easier said than done. During those times when I've stopped reading the Bible every day, and I've let the daily pressures of life eat away at my prayer time, I find that I forget to look to the Light for the solution to my problem. I forget to praise the Lord for the trials in my life that bring me closer to Him and only see them as another difficulty to slog through on my own. I turn my back on Christ, who is shining His light during the dark times. But when I stop and pray, turning to God for my peace and strength, then I feel His guiding hand on my life again and no matter what the storm is in my life, I feel as if, with God's help, I can conquer it, and even learn from it.

Dear Lord, Be my shining light, like that of a lighthouse, which illuminates dangers invisible to us without Your perspective. Guide me through all of life's trials. Remind me to turn to You first when any difficulty arises. Keep my trust and faith in You. Help me to remember and truly believe that You have a plan and purpose for my life. Align my will to Yours and enable me to learn from the tests that come my way so that I may grow closer to You and grow to be more like You each day. Amen.

SAND IN MY SHEETS

*Let the word of Christ dwell in you richly, teaching
and admonishing one another in all wisdom,
singing psalms and hymns and spiritual songs,
singing with thankfulness in your hearts to God.*

COLOSSIANS 3:16

Sand is great. It's so wonderful to take off my shoes for the first time each year, and go walking barefoot on the beach. The feeling of cool sand surrounding my feet is just magical. I love the way it cushions my feet, and acts like a fine piece of sandpaper on my rough feet. It's fun to have a seat on the sand and wiggle my toes around in its cool depths.

When living at the beach, even for a week, that sand inevitably starts migrating off the beach and into areas that I prefer for it to not be. For example, I can deal with sand in the front hallway; I'll just sweep it up. But when it makes its way into my bed because I wasn't careful enough to make sure all the sand was off my feet before I hopped into bed, then it starts to become a little irritating. Because, before I know it the sand is all over in my sheets and I wake up with a piece in my ear or molded to my face, or even worse, in my mouth or my eye.

One piece of sand in my mouth is almost as bad as crunching on a stray sin of omission. At first it's not so noticeable. I think, "Oh, I don't need to pray tonight, I'm tired. I'll pray in the morning." Or I might say to myself "I worked hard all day, instead of reading the Bible tonight I'll watch a movie." These decisions are like insidious pieces of sand that start to collect in my sheets. Once I stop intentionally walking with God, I unintentionally start wandering off His path. If I've been walking closely with God, these changes are easier to detect and will bother me more than if I haven't been walking very closely with Him. The further away we are from the Lord, the closer we are in and with the world, which tends to convince us that what we're doing isn't all that bad.

I once heard a great saying I've never forgotten and I often think of my life in this manner, "You're either growing in your faith or you're falling away." As I "see" my life in my mind's eye I can see God and me walking down a path, and if I'm not walking right next to God, in His Will, then I'm off the path and slowly getting farther and farther away from him.

No one ever falls away from God overnight. We don't just wake up and say "I'm going to wander away from the Lord's Will for my life." Instead, it's almost imperceptibly small steps that we take, or fail to take. I think for most of us it's really the sins of omission that are what sneak into our lives. I start doing yoga instead of having my quiet time; I surf the internet instead of using my time wisely to read a book that will help me grow in my faith. In and of themselves these things aren't bad, but when they start replacing my time with the Lord, then I have placed their importance before God and they've become my idols. Now, if I pray while I'm doing yoga or listen to Christian music in the background while I'm looking around the internet then I'm keeping my focus on the Lord, throughout my day. Because of our busy schedules and need to often multitask, I look for ways to carry God with me during my day. Maybe I hum hymns in the shower or pray while standing in line at the post office. In what ways can you keep close to the Lord in the middle of your days?

Dear Lord, It is so easy to let bad habits pile up to the point that I feel far away from You. Please help me to find ways to stay close to You by making You a part of my daily life, moment by moment, praying throughout the day and by using times that I'm just waiting in line, to talk with You, read Your word and praise You for Your awesome blessings in my life. Please keep me aware of areas in my life where I'm making bad choices, choices that lead me away from You, and help me to make choices for You instead. Amen.

BEACH GLASS

Bring the full tithe into the storehouse, that there may be food in my house. And thereby put me to the test, says the Lord of hosts, if I will not open the windows of heaven for you and pour down for you a blessing until there is no more need.

MALACHI 3:10

I love the smooth look and feel of beach glass and the way light shines through it. During my lifetime I've spent a great deal of time looking for beach glass on beaches around the world. Sometimes I would stay on the beach, searching for at least one piece of beach glass before I would allow myself to go in for the day, not satisfied until I'd found a piece.

There are so many different colors. Clear is usually the most abundant, followed by green. Then there are the brown and blue pieces. I have numerous clear glass jars full of it, decorating my home. But it's not as easy to find as it used to be because most soda today is found in aluminum cans instead of glass bottles, so less of it is being tossed into bodies of water. Being able to find beach glass is much like developing the skill to find a dry Petoskey on the beach. It takes practice, time and patience.

I think being able to find beach glass is like being able to see God's blessings in our lives. Sometimes it is hard to spot. But the more time you spend looking for ways that God has blessed you, the more you find. And all of a sudden you're just surrounded by a sea of blessings you didn't know you had.

Have you ever done an exercise where you write down all the things you're thankful for? Or written down a list of blessings you can see in your life? It's a great exercise in being grateful, and helps us to start thinking about the many ways in which God has blessed us. Whenever I start this exercise I occasionally get started slowly but then I have more ideas in my head than I can write down before I forget them!

God's blessing are so abundant! And even that little challenge you're experiencing right now – that can be a blessing too, if you are able to learn the lesson from it that God is attempting to teach you from it. If you're having a difficult time with something you suspect God is sending your way as a blessing, pray that He align your will to His Will, and pretty soon you'll see your attitude and perspective change to embrace it.

I've seen blessings come in the middle of the most challenging times of my life, such as when my sister was dying from cancer. That was such a difficult time, but full of blessings. God's strength, grace, and love were all around me in the form of friends and family, and my faith was deepened as I reached out to God, knowing that I wouldn't be able to make it through without Him.

Look for the blessings in your life and before you know it you'll be surrounded, by God's love, and His unending abundance.

Dear Lord, Teach me to look for the blessings that You've poured into my life which are so much more precious and beautiful than beach glass. Help me learn to have a grateful heart, and to appreciate and learn from the blessings You've sent my way in the midst of life's difficulties. Amen.

Sandcastles

But everyone who hears these words of mine and does not put them into practice is like a foolish man who built his house on sand. The rain came down, the streams rose, and the winds blew and beat against that house, and it fell with a great crash.

Matthew 7:26-27 NIV 2011

Sandcastles are a lot of fun to build, especially during a beach carnival. There's nothing like a little competition to get those creative juices flowing: black sand for the road to the castle, little pebbles to line the edges of the drive, beach grass planted around the edge to act as landscaping. And a moat - it's not a great castle without a moat, filled with water of course! Steps carved into the side of the tower and some clear beach glass for windows.

But sandcastles crumble. The water we used to hold the sand particles together dries out and our walls start to crumble. The water in our moat all too quickly is absorbed into the sand and it goes dry. Or, the worst of all fates, either a rogue waves crashes in, taking out all your hard work in a heartbeat, or a rogue child runs through your creation like Godzilla. And poof, it's all gone.

Sandcastles are temporary, like our lives here on earth. Sometimes we forget we're visitors here and that what we are experiencing now is just the "pre-life." How easy it is to get wrapped up in this world. We get busy outfitting and decorating our own personal sandcastles - the ones we live in, or drive. We spend time picking out just the right chandelier, or paint color for the living room walls, or bedspread to match the carpet. Not that these things are bad in and of themselves, it's just when they become the focus of our lives to the detriment of more significant pursuits, that they become our idols. We often spend too much time decorating our homes, making things "just so," accumulating wealth and worrying about what the neighbors will think.

Our focus and foundation needs to be on the Lord and He'll take care of the rest of our needs. Matthew 6:21 says "Wherever your treasure is, there the desires of your heart will also be." It is so important that our treasure be in the Lord, and in His love for us; in spending time with Him, in His word and getting to know who He is. Everything else, the things of this world, are just temporary. There's nothing of this world we can take from this world into the next.

What are the sandcastles in your life? Identify them, make a plan to reduce the importance they hold in your life, and seek to know the Lord more deeply each day.

Dear Lord, It is so hard to keep focused on the right things in this modern life. Please give me wisdom to see what is worthless in Your eyes, the strength to banish any idols in my life, and the steadfastness to read Your word daily and to keep You in the forefront of my mind each day, all day. Amen.

OPEN WINDOW

He makes me lie down in green pastures,
He leads me besides still waters;
He restores my soul.

PSALM 23: 2-3

When you arrive at the beach there's nothing better than getting to your beach front room, throwing open the window and enjoying that awesome breeze, fresh off the lake, and hearing the rhythmic crashing of the waves. It's so relaxing, invigorating, and refreshing, all at the same time. Ahh, I can just feel the white cotton chenille bedspread, cool in the fresh air, calling to me to come take a nap before the open window. "Come, and be refreshed," it says, "Come lay down for a refreshing nap!" it calls to me. I'm at the beach, why not take a nap?

What is it about the beach that calls us to relax, kick back, and enjoy life? Why does it entice us to take off our watches and keep a more relaxed schedule? I think part of it is that we're closer to God's awesome nature, and farther away from the every day routine of our lives. Usually we're on vacation, when our responsibilities lessen, even if only for a short amount of time.

This "voice" that the beach seems to have, the one that calls me to be good to myself and spend time getting rejuvenated, I think, is really my yearning to be closer to God. We spend so much time working at our careers, taking care of the chores, the house, the kids etc., that when we do have time to relax we're so exhausted that the only thing we can muster the energy to do is sit in front of the television and numbly absorb some show that is mildly entertaining but ends up leaving us feeling empty inside.

When I've taken that extra effort to shut off the TV, and open my Bible, or sit down to listen to a devotional podcast from Charles Stanley or Greg Laurie (two of my favorite preachers that have iPhone apps), I get rejuvenated and afterwards I feel better. I've spent time with God, being fed His Word, and being reminded that He is with us through all of our trials, both big and small, and that He loves us so much! God is always there, just waiting to rejuvenate us, to lead us beside still waters and to restore our souls. That refreshing breeze of our Lord and Savior is always there, just on the other side of the window. All we have to do is open it and enjoy the refreshing and life-giving breath that He offers.

It's certainly easier to make good habits while on vacation because we're not being pulled in as many directions as we are in our everyday lives. Sure, it's easier to find time to read a book while sitting on the beach, or to pull out your Bible and spend an hour in the New Testament, than it is after dinner on a work-night, or after helping your kids with their homework. But it IS possible to take those good beach-habits back to our homes with us. It's all about priorities. And about trying, and trying again when we drift away.

Find what refreshes you and make a plan to refresh yourself with God daily. Maybe it's listening to Christian music while you drive to or from work. Maybe it's reading one chapter a day in the Bible (or even a paragraph). Whatever it is, ask God to help you succeed, and when you look back on your life from a point in the future, you'll find yourself feeling more at peace with the results, and closer to God.

Dear Lord, This world is so challenging and it is sometimes so hard to make the time to spend with You. Please help me take the lessons I learn at the beach, lessons about relaxing and enjoying quiet time with You, and apply them to my daily life. Please help me to keep the window to You open. Restore and rejuvenate my soul and spirit when I am struggling, and help me to keep reading Your Word. Amen.

SEAGULLS

Then Jonah prayed to the Lord his God from the belly of the fish, saying, "I called out to the Lord, out of my distress, and he answered me; out of the belly of Sheol I cried, and you heard my voice. For you cast me into the deep, into the heart of the seas, and the flood surrounded me; all your waves and your billows passed over me. Then I said, 'I am driven away from your sight; yet I shall again look upon your holy temple.' The waters closed in over me to take my life; the deep surrounded me; weeds were wrapped about my head ...

JONAH 2:1-10 ESV

Seagulls are fun to watch as they soar above the waves, sometimes missing the spray by just feet. It's fun to walk along the shore and try to sneak up on a flock of them and run at them so they take off all at once. On days when I have nothing planned, I enjoy sitting on the beach and staring out over the lake, watching the seagulls and imagining what it would be like to be able to fly. You know, just to be able to lift off just by thinking about it – no wings, no plane, just to be able to levitate above the ground and float over anything I wanted to.

Watching the seagulls starts me daydreaming about all the places I want to travel to and how I wish I didn't have to work for a living. I'd love to be able to sell all my belongings and take off on a one-way trip around the world, stopping in all the places on the map that sound interesting. Rent a car in Europe and head off in one direction without any particular destination in mind, stopping along the way to check out any church, building, or lane that looks interesting and makes me wonder what I might find at the end of it.

On the flip-side, these thoughts of adventure have a darker side. I'm usually thinking how nice it would be to leave all my responsibilities and stressors; how nice it would be to run away and leave it all behind. Some of my favorite books are the ones about people who do sell everything and take off on an extended trip. Sometimes they hike through South America, or buy a sailboat and sail around the world, or maybe just around the South Pacific. Whatever they do, they're leaving their everyday lives behind and looking for adventure.

While my husband and I would still like to head out for adventure some day, it's become clear to us, through a lot of prayer, that God has called us to a different life at this point in time. As much as I often think the main goal of life here on earth is about having fun and enjoying myself, I know that's not really true. The main goal is to glorify the Lord in all that we do, to follow His Will for our lives and to bring people to Christ.

If my husband and I ran off, shirked our responsibilities, and fulfilled only our own desires and dreams, chances are God isn't going to bless our path. And on top of it, if we avoid the challenges and heartaches that come with following His path for us, we'd be shallower people with shallow characters and we wouldn't reap all the amazing benefits God has planned for our lives. I know, sometimes that sounds like crazy talk, but I know from the difficulties I've already faced in my life that it's those hard times that strengthen my faith, deepen my love for Christ and help me to more clearly see what God is trying to do in my life. It makes me a better person, too. As much as I sometimes hate to admit it, because sometimes I feel like saying loudly, "Ok, enough already! I really can't take any more challenges. I'm tired of learning and growing. Can't life just be easy for a while?" I know that God has the best plan for my life. I just have to get on board with it, trust Him, and lean on Him in all circumstances.

Dear Lord, Sometimes life is just so draining and I just want to run away from it all and have fun instead of slogging through another challenge that's in my path. But I know You allow difficulties to come my way in order to help me to grow and deepen my faith and to draw me closer to You. Help me truly believe that You have the best plan for my life and enable me to rest in You, through whatever comes my way. And on days where I want to run away, remind me of the big picture and the real reason You've put me here on this earth. Amen.

SQUARE DANCING

And let us consider how to stir up one another to love and good works, not neglecting to meet together, as is the habit of some, but encouraging one another, and all the more as you see the Day drawing near.

HEBREWS 10:24-25

Square dancing is all about community and ritual. It is so much fun to dance the dances I've known since I was a kid, that I've memorized and could very well dance in my sleep. Now as an adult I am introducing my kids to them. I love these old tunes. The beat mingles in my brain with memories of boys I had a crush on; my heart pounding as they came nearer and we clasped hands to spin each other around. The square dances I recall, on the shores of Lake Michigan, were filled with friends and family. I knew most of the people dancing on the tennis courts and I even knew the staff that called the dances. They were voices I was so familiar with. The dancing became more than a dance, it was fellowship - a joyful time to celebrate being together - parents and grandparents watching on the sidelines and joining in on their favorites.

I see the square dance as a metaphor for Community and relationships; interacting with each other face to face instead of having our heads buried in our phones. When I was in Hong Kong riding their mass transit system, and everywhere I looked people had their eyes trained on the little piece of technology they held in their hands - playing games, surfing the web, texting each other, updating their Facebook pages. But none of them were interacting with anyone directly around them. It is so easy to turn to technology and use it as a substitute for real community. It seems easier, less threatening, and at the end of a draining day, sometimes it's all we have the energy to do.

I belonged to a small group Bible study when I lived in Texas. Sometimes on the Tuesday we met all I wanted to do was drive straight home from work and veg-out on the couch. But I can tell you that every time I went to meet with that wonderful group of women, it recharged my batteries and left me filled with the most wonderful sense of peace and fulfillment. Real community. People who know, love and accept me. There's nothing like it. And when I experience that awesome sense of community, it keeps me on the right path and keeps me "in" community. It's a battle sometimes. We run ourselves so ragged at work and keep such a frantic pace in life that we often don't feel up to seeing anyone at the end of a long day.

When I've made the effort to slow down, unplug from the world, and spend my time in pursuits the world would think worthless, that's when I am closest to the Lord. And that is when my longing for community kicks back in. It's as if the further I am from this world the closer I am to God and my real self.

Dear Lord, Help me to embrace community and long for fellowship, both with You and brothers and sisters in the Lord. Encourage me to be a light in this often-dark world, and to not be afraid to get engaged in the lives of those around me. Amen.

SINK THE STINK

*Restore me to the joy of your salvation
and grant me a willing spirit, to sustain me.*
PSALM 51:12 NIV 2011

Playing in the waves, making sandcastles, boogie boarding and lying on the beach are all such fun. And when I'm in the middle of them, I feel invigorated; the sun is shining, I may be sweating but I cool off in the lake. The air is fresh and life feels great and smells good.

But then once I've come home, an aroma starts to snake its way through the house if I leave my towel or swimsuit lying around and don't rinse it off or stick it in the washing machine. There are little organisms in the water, especially in salt water, that soon turn that great beach smell into something funky and stinky.

The same goes for my walk with the Lord. My walk can feel so refreshing one day but if I don't keep on top of it, all of a sudden my life seems to stink. It's faint at first, but the longer I wander down a road of my own choosing, the worse it gets.

Our spiritual lives require frequent replenishment to stay fresh; like a stream. If part of the stream gets cut off from the natural flow, green scum starts to build up and starts to smell. We need that daily flow of nutrients in the form of prayer and reading the Word, in order to keep goodness flowing in our lives.

In my life this seems to be a continual ebb and flow; one day I'm doing great and feel as if I'm in the Lord's will, and the following week I've drifted away, carried off by laziness or the world's priorities. And then once I've realized what's happened, I correct my course and get back into the stream.

I'm sure this pattern sounds familiar. I think it's been around since the big Fall. The Israelites went through it in the wilderness. The sin within our fallen selves continually fights with our redeemed selves. And I suspect we'll have that fight continually until we go to be with the Lord for eternity.

The key is noticing if I'm drifting off course, and finding the desire to get back on course. Sometimes when I've drifted away I start with a prayer asking God to help me desire to get closer to Him again. Because sometimes I just don't feel like making the effort.

Dear Lord, This life can be so hard. Thank You for your love and constant grace, because I need it so often. Thank You that you sent Your Son to die for our sins, so that you can forgive us each time we sin. When I drift away from You, even just a little, encourage me to draw near to You again by spending time in prayer and by reading Your Word. Bless me in my desire to walk in step with Your will for my life. Amen.

SUNGLASSES

But be careful. Don't let your heart be deceived so that you turn away from the Lord and serve and worship other gods.

DEUTERONOMY 11:16 NLT 2007

Sunglasses are necessary on sunny days, or at least a pair of glasses with lenses that get dark in the sun. Sometimes the sun is just too bright, making it hard to see, and a good pair of sunglasses can really help cut down on the glare, especially if those sunglasses have polarizing lenses.

Polarizing lenses cut the glare and allow us to see things we might not otherwise be able to see. When I'm up on the North Bluff looking down at the water, sometimes I can see big fish swimming around if I have my polarized glasses on. Those lenses cut the glare on the top of the water and I'm able to see into it. The same phenomenon happens when I'm taking photographs with my 35mm camera if I have a polarizing filter on; when I'm shooting through a window, I can turn the filter until the glare on the window disappears and I can see through the window to what is on the other side of it.

A polarizer often makes the world look a little better than it actually is; skies are deeper blue, the water is a prettier color, and trees and grass are a more lush green. When I'm out for a walk on the beach and I'm thinking to myself "Wow, it's really beautiful out here – the colors today are amazing," I'll do a little test and pull my glasses far enough down my nose that I can see (although fuzzily) that the world without my glasses isn't quite the stunning color that I've been seeing through the lenses of my glasses.

Life with God is kind of like a polarizing filter. It takes this world and adds beauty to it. Experiencing this world through the eyes of faith takes a life that is unsaturated and dull and adds meaning and depth.

I've noticed that when I'm in the groove, and I'm praying throughout my days, talking to God in all circumstances and I'm really seeking His will for my life, it's then that life is looking pretty good, even if I'm going through challenges. I know that God is right there with me and that we'll get through it together. My life feels like it's in sharp focus and I'm enjoying the view. But when I've either stepped out of God's will or I've let the World take the front seat of what is most important in my life, it's then that my world starts to lose focus, seems dull and unsatisfying, and the World seems to create a glare which keeps me from seeing what is really important.

Dear Lord, Please enable me to keep on the polarizing filter of Your love; helping me to walk in Your Way throughout all my life. When I get blinded by the world, bring me back to You, help me to see the truth, and remember that You are the Way, the Truth and the Life. Amen.

VOLLEYBALL

Draw near to God, and he will draw near to you.

JAMES 4:8 ESV

Growing up at family camp in the summer, the conclusion of dinner meant one thing: Volleyball! In fact, we even had a little song we sang about it, to the tune of "Take Me Out to the Ballgame." This is the chorus:

> *Every night after supper*
> *Every night rain or shine*
> *We put up the net and play volleyball*
> *Of all the games 'tis the best game of all!*

Man, those were the days! Volleyball games at camp were so much fun. All ages played together and we didn't get too serious, but played hard and really had a great time together, as the sun started its descent over Lake Michigan.

There were several reasons I loved playing Volleyball at camp: I was a pretty good player, it was a tradition, and it often gave me a chance to face off at the net with whatever guy I happened to have a crush on that week.

But one week I got hurt. I'd gone up to the net to spike the ball at the other team, and another player on my team had done the same thing. We both wanted to be the one to make the play and neither one of us "called it." So, we weren't communicating and as a result, we ran into each other on the way down. His full weight came down on my ankle and I went down. I spent the rest of the week on crutches with my leg in a cast.

Sometimes, when we don't communicate during a game we experience the classic *faux pas* where everyone thinks someone else is going to get the ball and we all stand around looking at each other when it bounces on the ground right in front of someone.

Just as we need to communicate with our team members during a volleyball game, we also need to keep our communication flowing with God. We need to talk with Him. Even though He knows all our thoughts and actions, He still wants us to have daily conversations with Him, tell Him our worries and concerns, and ask Him for help through our trying times. He even wants us to praise and thank Him for all the ways in which He's blessed us.

God is the most important team member in our life. He is the one to whom we should invest the most time and have the closest relationship. In fact, the first commandment commands this of us. This is sometimes hard to remember or hard to comprehend, because, in one sense, He isn't visible to us.

In this modern, fast paced, frenetic world of ours, it's so easy to lose sight of what, and who is truly important. When I stop communicating with God is when I find myself getting hurt, getting into trouble and generally unhappy and frustrated. When I focus on daily prayer; keeping God the focus of my day by communicating with Him through prayer, throughout my day, I find that no obstacle is too hard to overcome because the Lord has provided me with His strength, His patience, and His peace. There's no better teammate than the Lord.

Dear Lord, Please keep my focus on You throughout my life. Urge me to turn to You in the midst of my busy day, asking for Your guidance, peace, and patience. Help me to keep our communication open and frequent. I love You so much. You are the best teammate in this life that I could ever pray for. Thank You for loving us so much that You sent Your only Son to die for our sins so that we can spend eternity with You in heaven. Amen.

Sunset

*"Martha, Martha," the Lord answered, "you are worried
and upset about many things, but few things are needed—or indeed
only one. Mary has chosen what is better, and it
will not be taken away from her."*

LUKE 10:41-42 NIV 2011

Sunset at the beach tends to be "an event." The best days at the beach have no schedule, no appointments, and nowhere you have to be at a certain time, until it's sunset time. Then it's almost like an impromptu party. People come out of their rooms, congregate on the patio or the porch, and they drink in God's amazing handiwork. Folks who live in a cottage along the beach invite their friends over for conversation and a drink. They pull out beach chairs, benches, odd card table chairs, and it's an informal gathering of neighbors there to commune with each other and with God.

One of my most memorable sunsets from this last summer was on the shores of Lake Michigan, in front of a tiny cottage down the street from our own cottage. I finally had made time to see the sunset on the last evening my friends were in town. I can still feel the warm glow of that evening in my soul. An hour or two of conversation, surrounded by nature and the spectacular sunset, we talked and laughed, accompanied by the rhythmic crashing of the waves in the background, until the evening chilled and we headed home to our beds. But the next day they left and I was left thinking to myself, "How come I only got around to this on their last night? That was awesome! I should have been there every night enjoying their company and fellowship!"

That's so often how we are about spending time with God. Oh, we want to, we say we're going to, and before we know it the summer has slipped through our fingers and we've allowed our schedules to stay too busy. The thing we want to do and should do most, we don't do. We haven't made it a priority. And we lose out.

God is always there for us waiting to bless us, waiting to talk and walk with us. But we have to be diligent in our walk with Him. Commit to spend time in the Word every day. Just like you make time to watch your favorite TV show. It's not that you're too busy, really, it's that you haven't given it a priority in your life. Challenge yourself to daily spend time in His word, to spend time talking with Him throughout each day, and to consult Him when you're tempted to let the world encroach on your "sunset events."

Dear Lord, My life is so busy and yet I yearn to spend time with You. Please help me to stay in Your word daily, and to prioritize the things You would have me put first in my life. And help me to see You in the natural beauty you've placed all around us. Amen.

BLACK FLIES

*No temptation has overtaken you that is not common to man.
God is faithful, and He will not let you be tempted beyond your
ability, but with the temptation He will also provide the way
of escape, that you may be able to endure it.*

1 CORINTHIANS 10:13

Summer on the beach can be marvelous – the sweet breezes, the crashing waves, time to sit in the sun and read a book or just to relax and do nothing. Beach combing is one of my favorite beach activities. I love to squat down in the sand along the water's edge and look at each rock that has piled up there, and of course, take some home in my pockets!

But sometimes a distraction comes along that can threaten to ruin the entire day, and my attitude. In Michigan one of the worst "plagues of the summer" can be the black flies, or any flies, really. When there is a rainstorm on the horizon they start biting and man do they hurt! It's not just annoying that they buzz around my head and valiantly try to fly into my mouth, but then their bite really starts to ruin my "beach zen." Or sometimes, on a really calm day, the mosquitos start to invade and before I know it my legs are a mass of itchy bumps that will take weeks to go away.

These irritations are like temptation in our lives. No matter how closely I am walking with the Lord, little enticements are constantly barraging my mind and my will. The lure of firing back a nasty-gram to that email that hit me wrong can be almost too much to resist. Or I might find myself wanting to be curt or sarcastic with one of my family members because they just asked me the same question for the 10th time. Then there is the temptation to ignore the world and salve my wounded soul in an hour of Facebook updates when I know there are other responsibilities just waiting to be taken care of. These temptations are like little flies buzzing around my head and there are days when it all just seems like too much to take.

Then in the midst of it all I take a deep breath to relax myself and turn my mind towards God. I tell Him what is bothering me, even though I know He already knows – He still wants me to talk to him. And I ask him to give me His strength, His peace, and to help me to do what I know I should do and not give into the temptation to be nasty. I ask that He give me perspective on the situation and allow me to choose my words carefully, to take emotion out of an email, or to let me feel that summer breeze in my soul that will allow me to keep doing all things in a way that would be pleasing to God.

Do you have a situation that seems to have crawled under your skin? Is someone bothering you by the way they're acting? Stop whatever you're doing right now and bring it to the Lord. Even if you don't feel like it – in fact that's the perfect time to do it. Tell the Lord what is on your heart and ask Him to help you. Before you know it your feelings will start to change and your perspective and outlook will improve.

> *Dear Lord, When I'm feeling irritated and annoyed by someone or something in my life and I'm imagining all the ungodly ways I'd like to respond, please work in my heart and in my mind to help me resist the temptation to be mean, unkind or rude. Grant me Your wisdom, Your peace, and Your strength to do what You would have me do. And allow me to see how You work in my life in response to this prayer. Amen.*

THE DINING ROOM

*For where two or three are gathered in my name,
there am I among them.*

MATTHEW 18:20

At the family camp I grew up attending meals were served in the communal dining room at scheduled times. Five minutes before the doors to the dining room were opened, a bell would ring from a central location and guests in camp would wander towards the dining room in anticipation of their next yummy meal. As a child I congregated around the door with the other children, eager to be let in first so I could try to figure out what we were going to be served.

Our one week at family camp was the one week during the year that I felt as if I was free; free from having to tell my mom where I was going to be at all times. Because the boundaries of the camp were well defined and because it was located in a tiny town, I think my mother felt I would be safe to go wherever I pleased as long as I stayed on camp property. She would know I was safe four times a day: at each meal, and at bedtime when she tucked me in. She also knew that because the guests at camp came year after year, most of us knew each other and she knew that most parents kept an eye open for everyone else's children in addition to their own.

That's one of the benefits of community that we often lack in our lives today. Most of us have moved away from home and do not live by family. Most of us do not have extended family living with us or even within driving distance. In the "old days" raising the family was a community affair and if "mom" wasn't immediately around, another mother could fill her shoes temporarily. Today we're often on our own.

Those times we all shared in the dining room were a form of fellowship; breaking bread together with other believers, and with families we'd known for decades. There's nothing like sharing a meal with someone to feel as if you really know each other. I'm always amazed at my job when I take the time to go out to lunch with someone. Afterwards I feel as if we now have a common bond and we're linked in a way we weren't before.

Breaking bread together - Jesus did it with His disciples. It connected them. Let's make sure we do it with other Christians. Invite a friend for lunch. Have a couple over for dinner. Go on a picnic with another family. Take the time to form those bonds and to fellowship with our Christian brothers and sisters. We're all going to be in Heaven together some day!

Dear Lord, Thank You so much for the opportunities we find to break bread together with other believers. Thank You for the amazing bond that is formed when we eat together and create in us a thirst to make new bonds with those we might not know well, and also to take the time to strengthen the bonds we have with old friends. Amen.

WALKING IN SAND

You shall walk in all the ways that the Lord your God has commanded you, that you may live, and that it may go well with you, and that you may live long in the land that you shall possess.

DEUTERONOMY 5:33

I love to walk on the beach. The part I like to walk on the most is that part right up close to the water, where the sand has been compressed and is slightly wet from the waves rolling up on shore, but it's far enough out of reach of the waves that I don't constantly have to be watching to see if I'm going to get wet. That sand is some of the easiest sand to walk on. It's firm and hard and my foot doesn't sink in the sand like it does farther up on the beach. Walking in the deep, dry sand can be really hard, and tough going, kind of like trying to walk up a sand dune – for every one step I take forward, I slip back almost as much.

When I am walking in-step with the Lord, my life can feel like I am walking in that good sand, the stuff that is easy to walk in. Life is enjoyable, difficulties seem easier to handle, and I can enjoy the walk instead of having to spend a lot of effort trying to get where I am going because the way feels like so much effort. You know how it feels when you're out for a walk with someone and your strides fall in sync? The walk becomes more enjoyable, and you start to feel like you've got a little groove going on. The journey feels easier. But when something distracts me and my stride falters, it breaks the groove and things start to feel all out of whack.

That's how it is in my Christian walk. I can be going along, walking in-sync with God, life is good, stressors aren't stressing me out, and then "bam!", I falter and my stride is off. I'm not feeling as close to God as I had been. I'm feeling off kilter and my peace has evaporated. That's the time, if I'm looking for a way back to God's presence, that I look around in my mind's eye to try to figure out what happened. I ask myself several questions such as:

- Have I stopped reading the Word daily?
- Have I stopped turning to the Lord throughout my day?

- Have I stopped praying regularly?
- Has something in my life become more important than God?
- Have I been too busy to spend time listening for God's voice?

And then I'll stop to pray.

Dear Lord, I feel as if I've drifted away from Your side. Your peace has left me and I'm feeling unsettled and disconnected from You. Please open my eyes to where I have drifted away from "the good sand." Send me Your peace, and restore my stride to match Yours. Keep me close to Your loving presence and hold me tight in Your sheltering arms. Encourage my heart and my mind to continue spending daily time in Your Word, and to look to Your loving guidance throughout my day. Amen.

SUNBURNS

*Of course, you get no credit for being patient if you are beaten
for doing wrong. But if you suffer for doing good
and endure it patiently, God is pleased with you.*

1 PETER 2:20 NLT 2007

Ahh, the first great beach day of the season and I'm excited to have time to sit on the beach, so I head down the road to my favorite little beach loaded up with all the accouterments I might possibly need: beach blanket, a good book, something to drink, sunglasses, hat, and sunscreen.

Applying sunscreen is a tricky business. It's so hard to make sure that all the spots I want covered have been covered so that I don't get burned. Inevitably I always miss a spot or two and I pay the price the next day and sometimes for days to come. I'm amazed at just how much a sunburn can hurt! Just like me, I'm sure you have stories about the infamous burn you got on your shoulders, the back of your knees, or inner thighs which was so painful you couldn't wear a shirt, a bra, or even let the sheet touch you while lying in bed. Sunburns hurt, and they can leave lasting damage, which shows up when we're older

Just like a sunburn hurts and smarts, so does persecution. And the sting of it can be just as surprising as getting burned by the sun. Those we know can lash out at us and inflict pain when we least expect it. The hardest pain to deal with is when I've just done something nice for someone or have done a good deed, and the recipient is unkind or wounds me by his or her words.

God says that we gain nothing by bearing punishment for something we've done wrong, but when we've done something good and are punished for it, God is pleased when we can endure it with grace and patience.

It's not easy. In fact, it's really hard for me to respond kindly when I feel I've been wronged. Proverbs 15:1 says, *"a soft answer turns away wrath, but a harsh word stirs up anger."* It's so true that if you repay unkindness with unkindness you create a vicious circle of anger and resentment.

Putting this principle into action has been one of the hardest lessons in my life. There is a person in my life that seems to always be looking for a fight; to say a nasty word in response to kindness. She likes to not only give me a sunburn, but rub Ben Gay on it as well.

I've said over and over to my husband, "I don't know how to not hate her. I don't know how to forgive her, to be nice to her nastiness. I don't know how to forgive her!" What I've realized since I met this person and have been searching for a way to be Christ-like to her is that I can't do it on my own; it's not in me. And it's not in any of us. Only through Christ and being close to God can any one of us respond as God would have us respond; in love.

I'm still working on it. It's a work in progress. But what I can tell you is that I pray for her every day, even if I don't feel like it. I pray that God would give her wisdom, and allow her to see the negative effect she has on others and for her to want to change and become a understanding and loving person. I ask God to forgive me for my unkind thoughts about her and I say out loud that I forgive her, even if I don't feel as if I really want to forgive her. There is power in saying the words. The words change my heart and I find that once I've said them, my heart follows, and I do mean them. On my good days I praise the Lord for bringing her into my life because she is a trial to me, and through it God is making me a stronger, better person, and is blessing me.

Dear Lord, Please forgive my anger when I'm wronged by others. Please enable me to use Your love and forgiveness to forgive others when they hurt me, even when they hurt me over and over again. Help me to respond to persecution with love, grace, and Your forgiveness. Give me Your strength to love others when they seem unlovable. Amen.

UNPLUG

Come to me, all you who are weary and burdened,
and I will give you rest.

MATTHEW 11:28 NIV 2011

Ahh, the beach! So often when I go to the beach I find that I unplug from the world. In fact, lately I've made it a requirement of any vacation. I want to go where I have no access to television, newspapers, internet, or even the radio. And the beach so often affords me that respite.

This world of ours seems to have its own standards, ones that are not my own, but ones that seem to creep into my life whether I want them to or not. I find myself updating my Facebook status when I'm somewhere fun or exciting, checking out where my friends are in the Find Friends app, and even playing a video game on my iPhone as I stand in line waiting to pay for groceries. This world has something available to occupy all of our time, without our even trying. In fact, the message that seems to be communicated through TV shows and magazines and news broadcasts is that if you're not plugged in you're missing out.

But what I find is that when I do unplug from this world, I can more easily focus on what is truly and eternally important – God. The lessons I learn at the beach are ones I carry with me back to the workplace, my home life and to my family. A walk on the beach, with only the sounds of waves crashing and seagulls overhead encourages me to be in the moment, not planning what needs to be done tomorrow. I find myself talking with God and spending time with Him instead of spinning my wheels worrying about things I have no control over. Because there is relatively no technology vying for my attention, I am free to be truly present with my friends and family; to smile at a sandcastle well made, or to exclaim over a Petoskey found hidden in the sand. And I can open my Bible to read more than a few verses without being interrupted by a phone call. I find myself pulling up an Adirondack chair on the patio and reading an entire book of the Bible, and enjoying it.

As I head back to my daily life I write a mental postcard to myself with some bullet points I want to remember when I'm in the middle of a busy day: • I can talk to God anywhere – make use of my commute and use it to listen to a devotional or talk to God • When waiting somewhere, read the Bible on my iPhone or pray for those on my prayer list • Turn off the TV. I'm sure you have your own ideas about what would be on your list. What do you want to remember from your time at the beach? Make a mental note about how much more at peace you feel when you commit to spending time with the Lord, and then commit to DO it. You might even send yourself a postcard at home with the main points you want to remember so that you can read them after you've returned to your daily life.

Lord, Thank You for the lessons of the beach and of nature. Thank You for time away from the distractions of this world; time when we can unplug from the world and plug into You. Thank You for Your grace and love, and for recharging my batteries daily, so that I can hear Your will for my life, and be open to accomplishing what You would have me do. Help me to keep this feeling of peace once I've left this place of rejuvenation, and encourage me to build in time where I'm unplugged from the world and directly plugged into You through Your word and in prayer. Amen.

RETREAT

Return to the Lord your God, for He is gracious and compassionate, slow to anger and abounding in love, and He relents from sending calamity.

JOEL 2:13 NIV 2011

L iving in the moment is so hard in our busy lives. A relaxing getaway is a wonderful way to recharge our weary batteries and get back to what is eternally important. I think the best vacations are the ones where I am able to unplug from everyday life. I leave my house with all of its to do lists and chores. I leave technology behind (well, mostly…), including newscasts and the internet and anything that gobbles up my time, and I enter a world where I have few responsibilities and no scheduled meetings.

It's then that I can focus on living in the moment; having time to stop, look into my husband's face and say "hello" and really connect with him instead of feeling like we only pass each other in the hallway on the way to check off another box on a long list of things we feel must get accomplished. How wonderful to sit down in an Adirondack chair with a book and a cold glass of iced tea, and have nothing else planned for the next two hours. It's fabulous to sit, feeling the breeze on my face and the warm sun on my legs and to not have my mind racing within me, trying to remember all the to do items I need to capture for the next day at the office.

It's then that life starts to feel real again and colors look more vibrant. I feel alive, invigorated, and I never want to leave this moment or this place. I've found my happy place. I thank the Lord for this moment and for all the blessings I so easily take for granted. Sometimes I feel like it's been a long time since I've connected with God, and it feels good to be having a conversation with Him. When I pick up the Bible, the passages are interesting and I find myself wanting to read more and more. I discover a passage I don't remember ever coming across and I wonder how I've missed it all these years. If I'm vacationing in a community where I know folks, I start to feel the urge to reconnect with people I haven't had time to visit with in what seems like forever.

I find it so funny that the process of slowing down seems to bring out the best in me; to reveal the real me. The wisdom of the world today preaches the opposite. "Go for it!" "Be all you can be!" "You can do it all!" The older I get the more I realize that the world's wisdom is flawed. It isn't wisdom at all; it's hype and it's marketing and it's just wrong, at least for me.

When I've learned to slow down and I've started creating good habits of talking with the Lord throughout my day, making time to read the Bible, and making time to cultivate friendships, I often find that I feel as if I'm smack dab in the middle of God's will for me. But it's so hard to hold on to when I return to my everyday life. I don't want to say goodbye to it; I want to hold it tightly and never let go. And yet, as I settle back into work and I mentally pick up my to do list, I eventually forget to hold tight to that conviction and slowly I let go of it and it's lost amongst the clutter of my life.

How do I hold onto the closeness with God that I cherish? How can I re-create a little of that retreat within my crazy life? It's certainly not as easy as it is when I'm away from most of my responsibilities, but I think, with God's help, it is possible.

Have you ever found that the things you make priorities tend to get done? If I make it a priority (even if it's only in my mind and not written down anywhere) to watch my favorite TV show, you can bet that I'll make time to do it. We just need to make God and reading His Word a priority in our lives. "I don't have time" only applies to things I don't value enough to make time for. Put "read Bible" on your to do list; make it a habit to say a prayer silently while waiting in line at the pharmacy or while stuck at a red light in traffic. And when you forget, just keep persevering. Ask God to help you make Him a priority in your life, and to nudge you back into the good habits you want to recapture from vacation.

> *Dear Lord, Sometimes this life is so challenging that I occasionally wish we could be in heaven with you right now. But until then, please help me feel You walking beside me each day. Turn me back to the good habits I want to cultivate and yet continually forget. Help me make time for You, keep You in my mind every step of my day, and nudge me when I have down-time, to use that time wisely, having a conversation with You. Amen.*

Now that you have finished, share with your friends!

Write a review on Amazon, Goodreads and other book-sharing sites,

and share your thoughts on Facebook.

Thank You!

Laura

ACKNOWLEDGEMENTS

This book would not exist if it were not for Carla Grebing, who encouraged me to write it. When Carla suggested I write this book it was towards the end of the summer and we were sitting along the shore of Lake Michigan watching another awe inspiring sunset with a number of friends gathered around in a semi-circle enjoying each other's company and the beauty that only God can create. Thank you Carla for the idea and for the encouragement and your firm belief that I could do it. What a wonderful project for the short, dim days of winter in northern Michigan.

The person who kept me motivated and encouraged throughout the entire process is my husband, Rob, who also provided my first edits. My whole life is enriched because of you.

And this book would not have been written were it not for my wonderful parents, who poured out their living faith into me from the time I was born. They gave me the firm foundation in Christ from which my faith continually grows. Thank you for your enthusiastic response to this project and your gusto with which you took on the task of editing.

A huge, heartfelt thank you to my life-long friend Beth Grimm, who so lovingly committed thoughtful time and effort into her edits, providing me with such inspiring suggestions. You are the grammar queen - and I love you for it!

I praise the Lord for His awesome blessings in my life, and for the lessons He teaches me every day. Thank you Lord, so much, for enabling me to capture in writing some of the lessons You have taught me. Please use these devotionals to bless the reader with with Your wisdom and empower them to apply these lessons to their lives. Amen.

ABOUT THE AUTHOR

Laura Vae Gatz was given a camera at a young age, and has yet to put it down. An avid adventure traveler, landscape and nature photographer and writer, Laura travels the world capturing word and visual images of culture, creatures, and the inevitable dialogue in one's head while traveling alone. Last year a friend pointed out to her that she'd traveled to all 7 continents in just 13 months. She's published a dozen coffee table photography books from her travels, available online. In 2009 Laura published a limited edition photo book of a vintage Christian family camp on the shores of Lake Michigan. In 2011 She published *Africa Via Antarctica*, the tales and photographs from her around the world, two-month sabbatical. *Beach Devotions* is her first devotional book - available on Amazon.com. Her most recent devotional is Autumn Devotions, published in 2015, also available on Amazon.

Laura lives with her husband, Rob, in Alto, Michigan.

84366237R00040

Made in the USA
Lexington, KY
21 March 2018